WOMEN OF VISION

IMOGEN CUNNINGHAM
1883-1976

WOMEN OF VISION

PHOTOGRAPHIC STATEMENTS BY TWENTY WOMEN PHOTOGRAPHERS

EDITED BY DIANORA NICCOLINI

INTRODUCTION BY ARLENE ALDA

The Unicorn Publishing House
New Jersey

My gratitude goes to the following:

In loving memory of my mother, Elaine Augsbury Niccolini,
who inspired me to live life with faith and hope and promise of fulfillment.

Arlene Alda for her valuable advice;

Angelo Lomeo for the title, *Women of Vision*;

Joe Scrocco and Jerry Raymond
without whose support this book would not have been possible;

Robert Sullivan, Jean Gruder and Joe Scrocco
for working endless hours on the details involved in the production of the book;

Stephanie Cohen for her sensitive portraits of the photographers;

Steve Brennan for his expert assistance and unfailing courtesy;

To each and every photographer included in this book,
and to Professional Women Photographers, I want to extend a very special thank you
for allowing me to work with such a great group of women photographers.

DIANORA NICCOLINI

Published by The Unicorn Publishing House, Inc., 90 Park Avenue, Verona, New Jersey 07044.

Printing History: First printing April 1982

Library of Congress Cataloging in Publication Data
Main entry under title:

Women of Vision.

1. Photography, Artistic. 2. Women photographers.
I. Niccolini, Dianora.
TR654.W65 779'.088042 82-81435
ISBN 0-88101-002-2 AACR2
IBSN 0-88101-003-0 (trade)

CONTENTS

INTRODUCTION

A collection of photographs by twenty different photographers can seem a little like a story in which each sentence is written by a different author. How do we achieve a unified statement?

I think the answer might lie in a different image.

Perhaps we are more like individual musicians in a symphony orchestra. Our singular tones blend into harmonies and counterpoints not possible when working alone. The tuba player recognizes that "oom-pah-pah," no matter how beautiful, is not the melody. We are all soloists—with cameras as our instruments—but by banding together we take on another identity. We all have different personalities, different training, different backgrounds, and are of different ages. As photographers, we feel comfortable shooting nature, animals, buildings, people and abstracts. Our pictures show design, color, texture, moment, interaction, drama, humor, pathos, beauty, imagination, insight and skill. We are photographers, yet poets; craftswomen, yet artists. Some of us are single, some married; some with children, some without. But taken all together, we reveal a certain unity. We communicate a resounding "yes" to what we consider to be a fullness of life.

In the short written statements that accompany our photographs, we reveal a little of the diversity of our lives—but also the concreteness of those lives.

We talk about celebrations, rejoicing, spiritual essences, fragile beauty, and the invisible. We also talk about simplicity, hours of labor, avoiding the laundromat and being fast and lucky. In eager tones Ruth Orkin says, "Look at this . . . look at that." Words, perhaps, symbolic of how down to earth we are.

And we are women.

How does our womanhood show in our photography? I tend to agree with Jill Freedman who says, "You can't tell the sex of the photographer by the photograph. A photograph is either good, bad or mediocre. . ."

But despite what I perceive to be the androgeny of our work, it is very important that we've come together as women. In doing so we make a statement of solidarity. We are joined together in an awareness of the sameness of our sex that not only allows for our individual differences, but celebrates them. We stand together as a group and let everyone know that women of accomplishment are proud of themselves and their contributions through photography. We take seriously our responsibility of role modeling. We've come from a long line of women photographers who have given us a history and have inspired us. We've taken from that rich storehouse, and we now give something back.

Yes, we are twenty photographers but our communication is of one voice. This is what we've seen. This is what we feel. These are our lives in these pages.

Arlene Alda

FOREWORD

Women of Vision is a visual statement by twenty contemporary women photographers reflecting the positive and creative aspects of life. I hope this book will not only be an important photographic anthology demonstrating the contribution of women to photography but a book that proves that it is not necessary to photograph the horrible, the ugly, the perverse in order to create good photographs.

As photographers we choose our subjects, thereby subjectively interpreting life and its complexities. It is our vision, or lack of vision, that distinguishes hope from despair. Interpretation is in our choice. Inspiration is our responsibility.

As the coordinator of the Professional Women Photographers, an organization whose purpose is to support and promote women in photography, I am particularly aware of the abundance of talent that exists among women in the photographic profession. I am also aware of the difficulties that many women have encountered and are still encountering, in lesser degrees, in trying to survive in a male-dominated profession. Only recently has the world acknowledged that women can be and are as talented and successful as men in fields other than nursing, teaching and secretarial work, that talent has nothing to do with gender. In the last decade women have taken their place in the arts, especially in photography. It almost appears as though photography has become a symbol of the new role of women in our society.

In *Women of Vision,* it is my intention to share with you a small part of the talent of women photographers. Because of the limitation of space, we include the work of only twenty women. Even if it had been possible to include 100 women photographers of repute, we would have hardly scratched the surface of the talent that exists. This book is not intended to be a comprehensive historical or international study of the work of women in photography. A book of that magnitude would reflect years of research. Instead this is a book of twenty contemporary New York women photographers whose work reflects its theme—*the fullness of life*. My decision to limit our selection geographically and thematically was because New York City is the cultural and photographic center of the world. Thus it was easy to find women photographers with international reputations without traveling too far. What was difficult was having to limit the selection to only twenty photographers. Because the selection was also influenced by the theme of the book, I chose only those women whose work is known for its positive, uplifting tenor. Each photographer was invited to submit photographs that she thought best expressed the theme. At the same time, each photographer was asked to write a brief statement describing her work in terms of the theme. These statements accompany the photographs in this book.

Women of Vision is dedicated to Imogen Cunningham, a great lady of photography, widely acclaimed for her portraits and for her exquisite photographs of plants and flowers. Her photographs seem to have transcended the boundary of time and captured the elusive qualities of that which is eternally beautiful and eternally present.

Jill Krementz is internationally known for her portraits of authors and other famous personalities. It is our good fortune that Ms. Krementz photographed Imogen Cunningham before her death and that she graciously allowed us to use one of these portraits in this book as a tribute to Cunningham.

Dianora Niccolini

RUTH ORKIN

My mother has said that when I was young I was constantly saying, "Look at this—Look at that." I think that taking pictures must be my way of asking people to "Look at this—Look at that." If my photographs make the viewer feel what I did when I first took them—"Isn't this funny . . . terrible . . . moving . . . beautiful?"—then I've accomplished my purpose.

Ruth Orkin, the daughter of a silent-film actress, grew up in Hollywood during the 1920s and 30s. During the heyday of the big picture magazines, she was a leading photojournalist. Ms. Orkin is also a film-maker. In 1953, she co-directed and co-wrote the award-winning feature film "Little Fugitive," for which she received an Academy Award nomination. In a 1959 poll of photography editors and critics, taken by the Professional Photographers of America, Ruth Orkin was voted one of the "Top Ten Women Photographers in the United States." Her first book, "A World Through My Window," published in 1978, was hailed by *The New York Times* as a "virtuoso performance." Her second book, a collection of her best work, "A Photojournal," was published in 1981. In reviewing "A Photojournal," Hilton Kramer wrote: "Ruth Orkin has long been recognized as a photographer of distinction . . . The wonderful picture of an American girl in Italy . . . is deservedly a classic."

1. American Girl in Florence, Italy, 1951 2. Kids Reading Comics, late 1940s 3. Jimmy the Storyteller, New York City, 1947 4. Opening Night Party of *Member of the Wedding*, Ethel Waters, Carson McCullers and Julie Harris, 1950 5. Hollywood Bowl Easter Sunrise Services, 1948

America Sings
Harmony Hymns
In keeping with the President's request, we too have reduced prices as much as
20%

SUZANNE SZASZ

Most women attain immortality by having children; unable to do so, I found mine in photographing children.

As often as I could, I followed the life of individual children, to document their development and assuage my curiosity. In 1955, I had an assignment to photograph a baby's first year. Twenty-five years later, I am still interested in Chrissy. It is hard to show so many years on a few pages; and many times I had to miss long months or even years without being able to see her. But if I could show you about 100 photographs of Chrissy, you would get to know her and also understand how she and the other 1,200 children I photographed have added to the meaning and fullness of my life.

Born and educated in Hungary, Suzanne Szasz came to America in 1946 and started photographing in 1949. Her picture stories and illustrations have appeared in many magazines and other publications, including *Life, Look, Saturday Evening Post, McCall's, Ladies' Home Journal, The New York Times Magazine, Esquire,* and *Parents Magazine.* Her first book, about children's everyday problems, was published in 1952 and was a forerunner of her ninth and most recent book, "The Body Language Of Children," with a foreword by Dr. Benjamin Spock.

Ms. Szasz has won several prizes for her picture essays and a number of art directors' awards for her advertising work. In 1980, Ms. Szasz began to exhibit her work in galleries and museums, and has quickly enjoyed five one-person shows, including a February 1982 exhibit at New York's Neikrug Gallery and an April 1982 retrospective at the National Art Gallery, in Budapest, Hungary.

Chrissy: 1. Four days old 2. A year and a half old
3. Three and a half years old 4. Nine years old 5. Sixteen years old

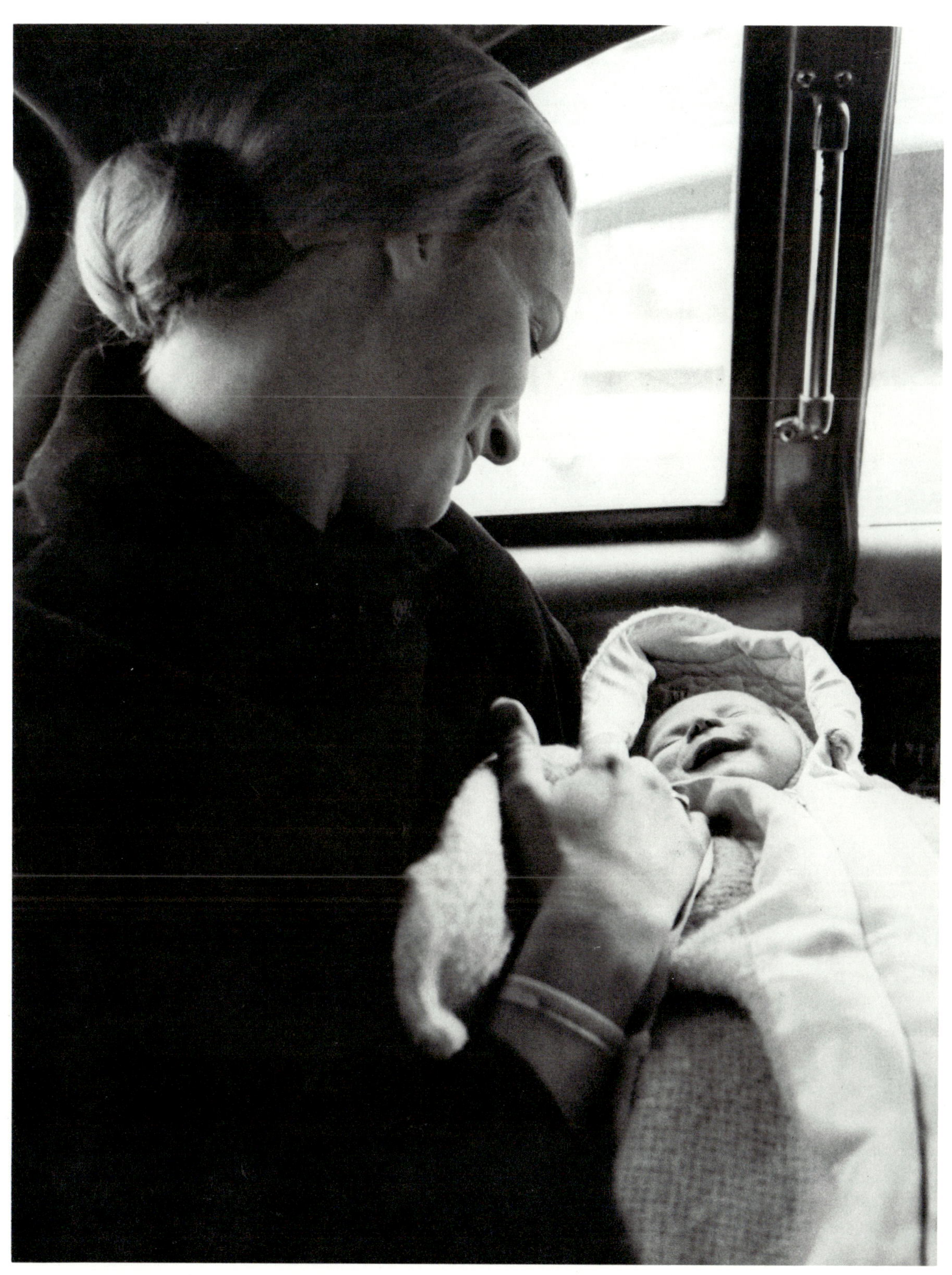

FRANCES McLAUGHLIN-GILL

For me a photograph is a happening where often the scene is set before I know that it is occurring. Such a photograph is "The Tent Makers," which I made on a foggy, wet summer evening. I was in charge of my sister's children and my three-year-old daughter. While I was in the house the children stole away to the beach, taking *every* blanket with them to make a crazy-quilt tent. When I suddenly missed them, there I found them in the tent. Sensing that this was a never-to-be-repeated event, I grabbed my camera and made the photograph . . . a photograph that speaks of dreams and wonder, of memory and hope. A photographer who is lucky is there with her camera at the precise moment.

Frances McLaughlin-Gill, a freelance photographer, began her career in 1943 as staff photographer for the Condé Nast Publications. Her work has appeared in many magazines, including *Vogue, Glamour* and *Town and Country,* and has been exhibited widely in galleries and museums. Ms. Gill's photographs were included in the shows "Photography in the Fine Arts I and II," which appeared at the Metropolitan Museum of Art in 1962 and 1964 and, most recently, at the Neikrug Gallery in New York. She co-authored, with her twin sister, Kathryn Abbe, "Twins On Twins," and, with Jane Safer, "Spirals From The Sea: An Anthropological Look at Shells."

1. Riverboat Gamblers, 1979 2. Beth and Harriet Troxell, Gymnasts, 1979
3. Marilyn and Rosalyn Borden, 1979 4. The Dancing Class, 1947 5. The Tent Makers, 1961

GG
GG

OCCUPIED
OCCUPIED

BARBARA MORGAN

From pre-historic times, the human psyche has found inspiration in art expression, from cave paintings then—to film and photography now.

Art externalizes our human responses to the intensities of life: visually, verbally, musically and kinetically, through the creative spark—echoing, experimenting and harmonizing our life forces into life fulfillment.

Barbara Morgan first studied and taught drawing and painting at UCLA. In 1935, influenced by the work of Edward Weston, she turned to photography. With the publication in 1941 of her first book, "Martha Graham: Sixteen Dances in Photographs," Ms. Morgan established herself among the nation's most important photographers. She continues to be known for her photographic studies of dance. Her work is included in such collections as those of the Museum of Modern Art and Metropolitan Museum of Art in New York and the Smithsonian Institution in Washington, D.C. At age 81, Ms. Morgan continues to exhibit, lecture and teach. She is revered as one of the seminal figures in American photography.

1. El Flagellante, 1940 2. Girls Dancing by the Lake, 1945 3. Children Singing in the Rain, 1950 4. Piglets Nursing, 1960 5. Bear Hugging, 1946

ERIKA STONE

Photography has indeed filled my life—filled it with endless visual excitement, as well as the challenge and satisfaction of getting moments which have tickled my vision on film.

So many subjects inspire me or strike a visual chord in me that I find it difficult to concentrate my work in a single area. Yet nothing compares with the thrill I experience when I capture a special moment in the life of a man, woman or child. People are my favorite subject and I marvel at the diversity of mankind and the uniqueness of each individual.

Although I stray sometimes, I always come back to photographing people. They, to me, give life its fullness; its richness. Their sorrows fill me with compassion; their joys move me deeply. To me, people are what the world is all about. That is why my camera will always seek them out.

Erika Stone's documentary photographs reflect her long and active career as a photojournalist and magazine photographer. Ms. Stone was a member of the legendary Photo League in the 1940s when, at age seventeen, she photographed her famous "Bowery Series," a photo essay on the people and life of New York's Bowery district. She later studied photography with the renowned Berenice Abbott and George Tice. Her work has earned many awards and has been widely exhibited.

Ms. Stone has specialized in photographing children and family life and her work has been seen in such publications as *Life, Time, Parents,* and *Ladies' Home Journal* and has been used in books by such publishers as McGraw-Hill, Simon & Schuster, Harcourt Brace Jovanovich, Grolier and Houghton-Mifflin. Ms. Stone has illustrated several children's books, including "Learning For Little Kids."

1. Mirage 2. Danny Kaye at Tanglewood 3. Rita Gam and Marlene Dietrich at the Circus 4. Bowery Beauties, 1942 5. Test of Strength, 1942

MONTE CARLO
World-Telegram
It Happened Last Night
Daily

KATHRYN ABBE

My photographs are, and always will be, celebrations of the simplest events of life. During the forty years that I have worked, certain visions have danced in my head: eyes full of wonder, holidays, birthday parties, the changing seasons, the relationship between children and animals. When I see the moment, I get a message from the color, the light and the gestures of people. I know when it "feels" right: I have learned not to count my pictures until the negatives are printed. There are many disappointments, but also happy surprises in photography. With Hasselblad and Nikon I have documented the fleeting moments of friends, family and strangers.

Kathryn Abbe, a graduate of Pratt Institute, worked for two years for *Vogue* photographer, Toni Frissell, and, since 1945, has had photographs published in such publications as *McCall's, Good Housekeeping, Better Homes and Gardens,* and *Paris Match*. Her work has been exhibited at the Metropolitan Museum of Art and the Brooklyn Museum. With her twin sister, Frances McLaughlin-Gill, she co-authored the book "Twins On Twins." Ms. Abbe's photographs of twins have been exhibited at the Neikrug Gallery in New York and the Guild Hall in Easthampton, New York.

1. Leslaw and Waclaw Janicki, twin actors, 1979 2. Laughing Horse, 1978
3. Bubble Gum Machine, 1980 4. Vivian and Marian Brown, San Francisco twins, 1979
5. Dancing at the Wedding, 1981

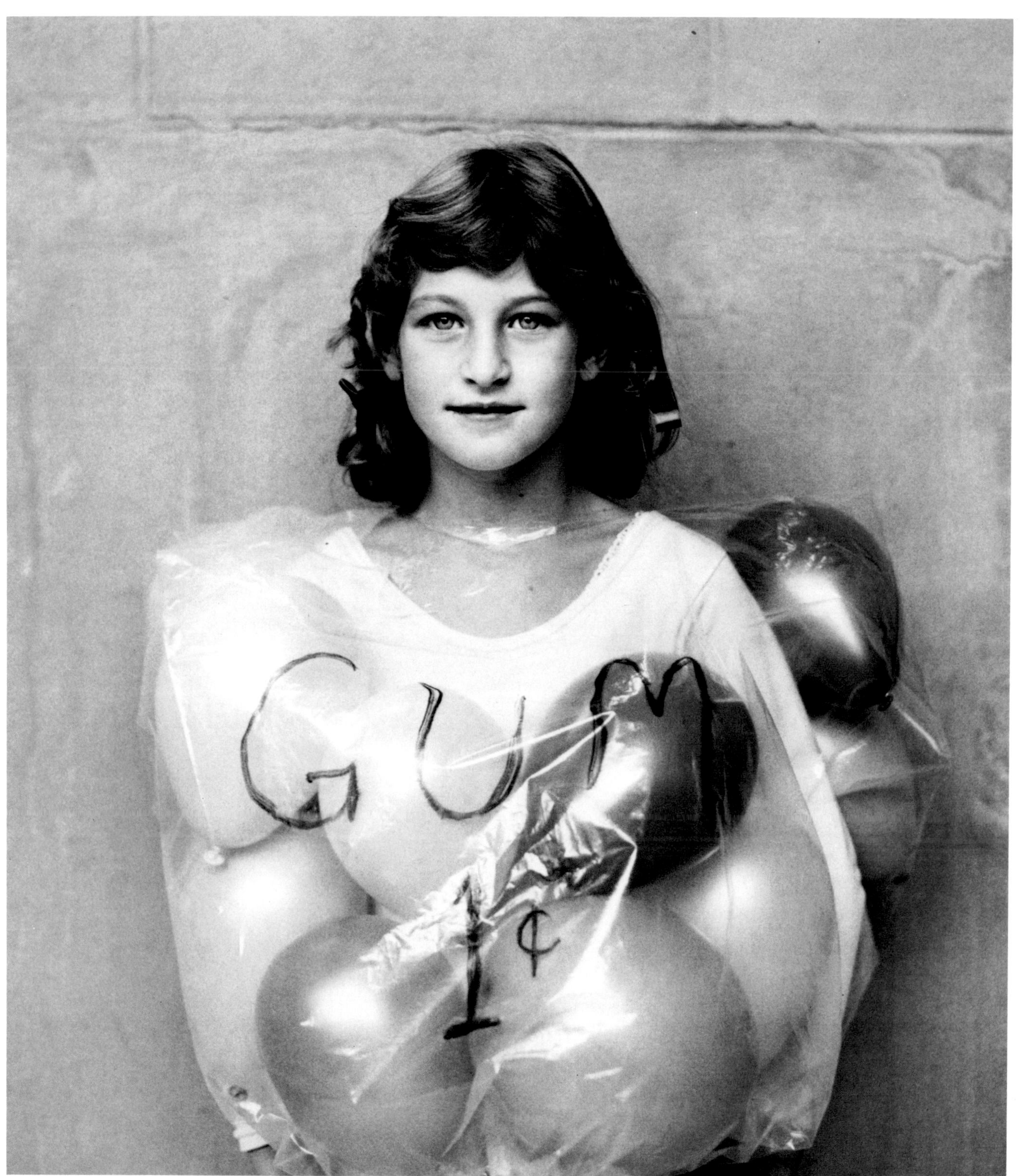
GUM
1¢

JILL FREEDMAN

You can't tell the sex of the photographer by the photograph. A photographer is either good, bad or mediocre, male or female. A good picture is one that works. It works if you have communicated or shared an idea or feeling. It is a way of saying—Hey, look at this. So you have to be fast and you have to be lucky.

Jill Freedman was born in Pittsburgh, Pennsylvania, and studied sociology and anthropology at the University of Pittsburgh. Before turning to photojournalism, she was a successful folk singer. Her photographs have been published in many books and periodicals, including *Life, Look, Geo, Time, Newsweek, Esquire, Time-Life Books, The New York Times* and *The London Times.* Ms. Freedman has created several photographic books, including "Firehouse," "Circus Days," "Old News: Resurrection City" and her latest book, "Street Cops," which has won her critical acclaim not only as a photographer but as a writer as well. Her work has been widely exhibited in the United States and abroad.

1. Roseland Matinee, 1976 2. The Total Woman, 1975 3. Toga Dance, 1978
4. Hector, 1972 5. Mabel, 1977

STEPS
OF

LIDA MOSER

Besides photographing that which is beautiful, which is about love, growth, fulfillment, I yearn to capture the invisible, the breath of life, the heart-beat, and by whatever means; magic, technique, and passion to strive to get it through the lens and onto the film—and if this warm glow stays alive and seeps onto the photograph (be it quiet, or gentle, or laughing, or loud) and is transmitted to the viewers, and seen and felt by them, then you really have something, and it is a great, gorgeous feeling for everyone—strength-giving—like an embrace, a hug, a reinforcement.

I believe that's what this book and the pictures in it are all about.

Lida Moser started her photographic career working with Berenice Abbott organizing Abbott's collection of Eugene Atget's negatives and prints. Later, a *Vogue* assignment sent Ms. Moser to Montreal, where she photographed her famous "Quebec Diary, 1950." Her photographs have been widely exhibited and are in a number of major collections. A book of her Quebec photographs was published in 1982.

For more than ten years, Ms. Moser has written articles on photography for the Arts & Leisure section of *The New York Times.* In addition, she is the author of many books, including, "The Amphoto Guide to Special Effects," "Grants in Photography," and "Contests in Photography." Her work has been used on the covers of many paperback books published by Bantam, Avon, Dell and Pocket Books, and in numerous magazines and periodicals, such as *Look, U.S. Camera, Vogue, Woman's Day* and *London Illustrated*.

1. Aaron Siskind, 1949   2. Danny Clark, 1976   3. The Dotzlers, 1954
4. Pawel Checinski, 1976   5. Leonard John Crofoot Studying a Painting by John Koch, 1975

NOEL

VIA WYNROTH

The dead and the living, men, beasts, and gods,
trees and stars, and rivers, and sun and moon dance through
the region of myths . . . where everything may be anything,
where nature has no laws and imagination no limits.

Andrew Lang

One often can't immediately comprehend the attractions, the play, but like the former child that collected treasures in her pockets for safekeeping, images are a gathering of pieces that hold my world together.

In the sea of discards, these attempts are a beginning toward that unsolved puzzle.

Via Wynroth is Director of Education at the International Center of Photography in New York. She has directed its education programs since the Center was created in 1974. Ms. Wynroth received her Master of Fine Arts degree from the School of the Art Institute of Chicago and is the author of the book, "The Looking Glass," which evolved from a project at a half-way house and an old-age home. She is now on sabbatical leave from the International Center of Photography, living in a log cabin and working on several children's projects.

1. Chicago, 1979 2. Loch Ness, Scotland, 1980 3. Saugerties, New York, 1981
4. *Diana-on-the-run* series, 1978 5. *Diana-on-the-run* series, 1978

SONJA BULLATY

My language is photography not words. In a world of much pain and confusion, perhaps in spite of it, my theme is the celebration of life and being part of its wonder.

I try to see a leaf as for the first time, to discover its fragile beauty before it dies to nourish the earth anew; I try to capture the growth of a tree as it reaches for the sun; I try to record the brief moment when the firepink brings color to the forest green, or the deep snow of winter gives way to a blustery March day.

Perhaps the one certainty in life that I always come back to and that I find most reassuring is the knowledge of constant change; the certainty that spring will return . . .

Sonja Bullaty, born in Prague, Czechoslovakia, lives in New York City with her husband, Angelo Lomeo. Working individually and together, they are masters of the art of color and black and white photography. Their photographic essays have appeared in many major publications, including *Camera 35, Popular Photography, Modern Photography, Life, Horticulture, Horizon,* and *Country Journal* and have been published in four volumes of the "Time-Life Wilderness Library," the "Audubon Tree Guide," and their own book, "Vermont in all Weathers." Ms. Bullaty's work has been widely exhibited at many museums, including New York's Metropolitan Museum of Art and Museum of Modern Art, Massachusett's De Cordova Museum, and the Museum of Modern Art in São Paulo, Brazil.

1. Sunrise, Kaibab Forest, 1980 2. Firepinks, Great Smoky Mountains, 1974
3. Frosty Leaves, Vermont, 1976 4. Deep Snow, High Sierra, 1971
5. March Sunset, New York, 1976

ARLENE ALDA

What I do as a photographer is to see, react, and record. I do that whether I photograph a person, a leaf, or an animal. I feel so lucky because I can respond to a variety of stimuli in my environment. These responses make me feel alive and it's my desire to give back this life affirmation through my photographs.

Arlene Alda has been a photographer since 1968. In 1974 she received the Chicago Graphics Award for Excellence in the Communicating Arts for her photo essay entitled "Allison's Tonsillectomy." Her work has appeared in such publications as *The New York Times, New York, Pageant, Redbook, Saturday Evening Post, Today's Health* and *Ms.*, and she has had exhibitions in New York's Nikon House, Soho Gallery and Modernage Gallery. Ms. Alda's photographs have also been included in many books, including "Women Photograph Men" and "Broadway Musicals." She has created several books, mostly recently, "ABC, A New Way Of Seeing," a children's book using images to explore letters of the alphabet, and "On Set," a personal story with photographs from the set of the movie, "The Four Seasons."

1. Japanese Schoolchildren, 1981 2. Chinese Woman, 1981 3. Chestnut Vendor, Japan, 1981
4. Lotus Leaf, California 5. Swan, California

NANCY BROWN

I have been a professional photographer in New York City going on five years. Before opening our studio, my husband and I were professional models and taking pictures was our big outside interest. Most of my earlier work was outside on location using real people, my children and friends. Since we have been in our studio, I have been doing fashion and beauty photography as well as location work. I love taking pictures of people whether it be models or non-professionals and I also love the business even though it is highly competitive and at times a "little crazy." All in all, I feel very fortunate being able to combine what I really enjoy doing and how I make my living.

Nancy Brown, a former fashion model turned photographer, works with her husband, David Brown, also a former model. Her photographs have appeared in a number of popular publications, including *Woman's Day, Family Circle, Glamour* and *Redbook*. Ms. Brown has written several articles for *The Professional Photographer, Studio Photography Magazine* and *The New York Photo District News*. Ms. Brown's commercial photography has been directed principally towards advertising, with clients such as Helena Rubinstein, Avon and some of New York's top agencies. Her work has been exhibited at the Nikon Gallery in New York and at advertising agencies such as J. Walter Thompson and Compton.

1. Pennsylvania Dutch Man and Child, 1977 2. Shepherd, Germany, 1970
3. Man with Oxen, Holland, 1970 4. Laundry, Italy, 1970 5. Woman in Doorway, Italy, 1970

MARCIA KEEGAN

Photography is a way of life for me. My personal vision and philosophy direct the path of my work; photography is my means of sharing my personal beliefs, friends and experiences with others. I am most interested in those images that evoke, through beauty, the spiritual essence of human existence and of nature. Photography is a magical way of communicating with others and of communing with nature anywhere in the world.

Marcia Keegan has exhibited in museums and galleries throughout the world and is the author, photographer and designer of many photographic books, with subjects ranging from old vaudevillians living around Times Square in New York ("We Can Still Hear Them Clapping") to Tibetan Buddhism ("The Dalai Lama's Historical Visit to North America"). Ms. Keegan is best known for her photographs of Native Americans of the Southwest. In addition, she has illustrated two children's books, "Only the Moon and Me" and "Moonsong Lullaby." Ms. Keegan's photographs have been exhibited at many museums and galleries and are included in many collections, including the Library of Congress, the White House, and the Smithsonian Institution in Washington, D.C., and, in New York, the Metropolitan Museum of Art, Lincoln Center Museum of Performing Arts, Neikrug Gallery, and Witkin Gallery.

1. Taxco Street Scene in Mexico, 1971 2. Himalayan Goatherd, 1980
3. Classical Lawnmowing at the Taj Mahal, 1980 4. Floating Market of Dal Lake, Kashmir, 1980
5. Kashmiri Lotus Unfolding, 1980

TANA HOBAN

Whether I am photographing children or fruit or heavy machinery, I am always searching for the story of the light—its path and pattern—and how to make my statement in the simplest, most direct way. I hope by sharing my vision with the viewer, I in some way share the fullness of my life.

Tana Hoban received a John Frederick Lewis fellowship from Moore Institute of Art to study painting abroad. Upon her return, she took a course in photography which began her photographic career and she has been a free-lance photographer ever since. For the past eleven years, Ms. Hoban's career has largely concentrated on educational books for children. She is the author and photo-illustrator of fifteen books for children, including "Shapes And Things," "Look Again" and "Count and See." Ms. Hoban has received numerous awards for her books and photographs.

Ms. Hoban's photographs have been published and reviewed in numerous magazines, including *Life, Look, Vogue, Scientific American,* and *Ladies' Home Journal.* Her work is in the permanent collection of the Museum of Modern Art and was included in the museum's renowned exhibition, "The Family of Man."

1. Lemons in Wire Basket, 1981 2. Eggshells, 1981 3. Pebbles in Water, 1981
4. Peaches on a Paper Bag, 1980 5. Eggs in Wire Baskets, 1979

SUZANNE OPTON

Still Life Photos: "A exists and B exists and this is how they look and/or behave together." I use simple, ordinary elements. I start out systematically. But soon I lose my grip, and the process unfolding before my eyes carries me along. I'm fascinated by the edge between dramatic and melodramatic; I want to measure the distance; how far can I go before something humorous becomes something ridiculous? I love that I can participate in some of life's small dramatic moments, and that I can preserve them on film, proof that they existed.

Suzanne Opton has been the recipient of grants from the National Endowment for the Arts and the Vermont Council on the Arts. Her photographs have appeared in numerous newspapers and publications, including *Life, New York, Vermont Life, Esquire, The Village Voice* and *The New York Times* and portfolios of her work have been published in *Popular Photography Annual* and *35mm Magazine.* Ms. Opton's photographs also have appeared in several books, including, "Women Photograph Men," "Growing Old," "Family Of Children," and "Women See Men." She has exhibited at New York's Marcuse Pfeifer Gallery, Neikrug Gallery, International Center of Photography and Floating Foundation of Photography, among others.

1. Untitled, 1980 2. Untitled, 1978 3. Untitled, 1979
4. Untitled, 1980 5. Children Ever Born to Women Ever Married, 1981

MAGGIE SHERWOOD

The feeling of being a free bird has kept me photographing and printing. I break all the rules and let the creative juices flow ending up with a potpourri of photographs. Versatility is what I strive for and I can enjoy any form of photography. The 60s studying with David Vestal was the high point. He urged me on. The 70s—the Floating Foundation of Photography, teaching in the prisons—what great moments! I hope my future prints will sing with energy.

Maggie Sherwood started as a landscape and commercial portrait photographer. In 1970 she founded the Floating Foundation of Photography, a gallery and educational center moored in the Hudson River on the West Side of Manhattan from which she has produced many exhibitions and international traveling shows. Ms. Sherwood's teaching has brought photography to people of all ages—from pre-schoolers to senior citizens—in hospitals, psychiatric centers, schools and neighborhoods, and she initiated the first photography programs in women's prisons in New York.

Ms. Sherwood's photographs have been widely published, including portfolios in INFINITY, Famous Photographers Annual and other camera annuals. A pioneer in experimental photography, her work is in the collections of the Smithsonian Institution and Bibliothèque Nationale, as well as in many private collections.

1. Central Park Lake, 1969 2. Snowstorm, Garment Center, New York, 1965
3. Boardwalk, Atlantic City, 1963 4. Coney Island Ferris Wheel, 1961 5. Central Park Trees, 1962

IDE
WHIRL
A

DIANORA NICCOLINI

The particular way of being that gives something its nature, the combination of qualities making something what it is, this is life in its fullness, best expressed through the myriad forms found on our planet, both animate and inanimate. Form is the language of the universe singing its praises. Its rejoicing is seen everywhere—in the sun through a web of hair, in the flower and its petals, in the subtle folds of a garment, in the human body. Everywhere we see life expressing itself and rejoicing in its splendor.

Dianora Niccolini was born in Florence, Italy of an American mother and an Italian father. In 1974 Ms. Niccolini began to focus her camera on the more creative aspects of photography and it was not long after that her work was being reviewed in such publications as *The New York Times, Arts Magazine,* and *Popular Photography*. Her photographs have appeared in several photographic anthologies, including "Women See Men," "Women Photograph Men," "History of the Nude in Photography," "The Male Nude In Photography" and, most recently, "New American Nudes."

Ms. Niccolini is the Coordinator of Professional Women Photographers, a national organization whose purpose is to support and promote women in photography. She is listed in Marquis' "Who's Who In American Women" and "Who's Who In The East."

1. Sun through Web of Hair, 1974 2. Calla Lily, 1982 4. Fold and Form, 1982
4. Freesia, 1982 5. Gladioli, 1982

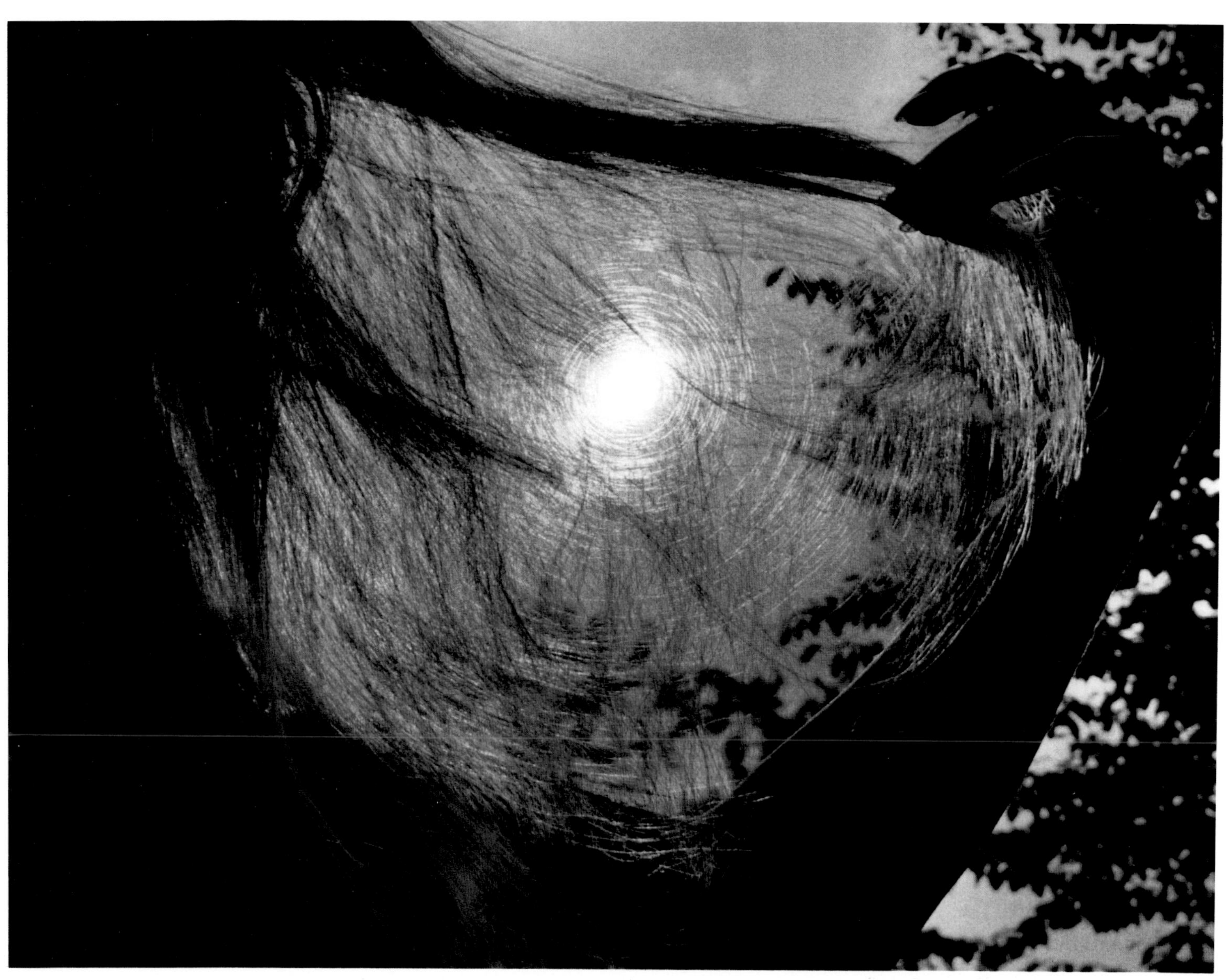

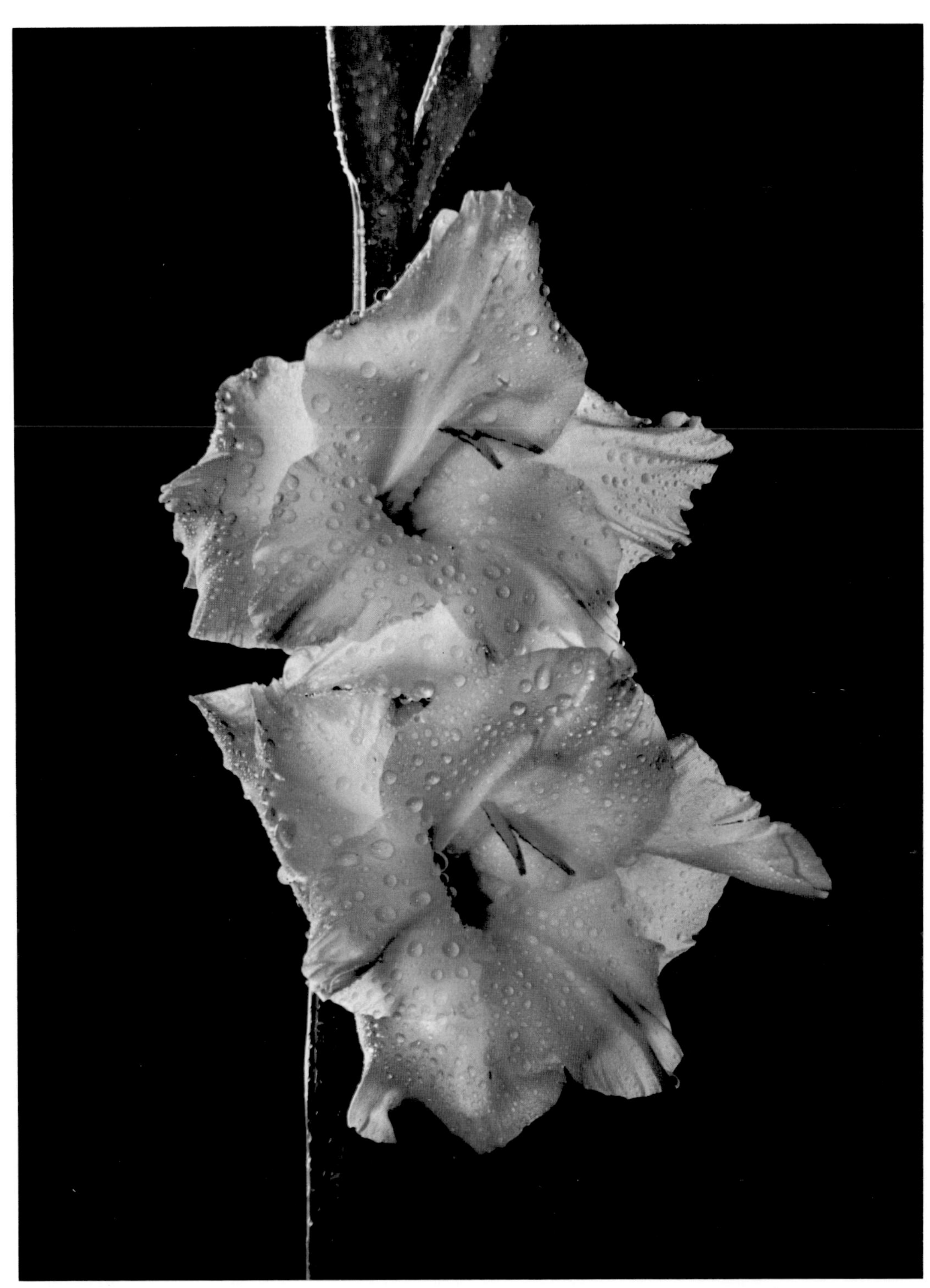

LILO RAYMOND

Photography for me is a way of avoiding grown-ups, boredom and going to the laundromat. It allows me to live in another world, intensified and of my own finding. I assume the right to stare long and hard, to be blunt, loving and unselfconscious. I attempt to find a kind of poetry that eludes me in other more sober activities. It has become a continuous search with no shining end in sight except to go on trying.

Lilo Raymond's photographs are included in the collections of the Museum of Modern Art and Metropolitan Museum of Art in New York, the New Orleans Museum of Art and the St. Louis Museum of Art. Her work has been exhibited in such places as New York's Helios Gallery, Willard Gallery, Floating Foundation of Photography and Marcuse Pfeifer Gallery, which has published a portfolio of her work. Ms. Raymond has been included in a number of reference books for photograph collectors and in several *U.S. Camera* and *Popular Photography* annuals. Her photographs have been published in many books, including "Country Inns of America," and "Family of Children." Her work has appeared and been reviewed in such magazines and newspapers as *Avenue, Country Living, House Beautiful, The New York Times,* and *The Village Voice.*

Ms. Raymond is also a distinguished teacher of photography at New York's School of Visual Arts, the International Center of Photography and the Maine Photographic Workshop.

1. Amagansett, 1977   2. Still Life, 1976   3. Pear, 1980
4. Franny, Roxbury, 1976   5. Franny, Warwick, 1973

EVA RUBINSTEIN

What is a photograph? For me, a fragment of quick-silver, a lucid dream, a scribbled note from the subconscious to be deciphered, perhaps, over years. It is a monologue trying to become a conversation, an offering, an alibi, a salute. It may attack, it may caress, express love or outrage, make political statements and explore one's vision of life and death. Given too much light, we are blinded—given too much shadow, we are lost. In the words of a poet, "The deepest thing I know is that I am living and dying at once. My commitment is to report the dialogue."

Born in Argentina, Eva Rubinstein spent much of her early life in Paris where she studied dance and theater. After the outbreak of World War II, she emigrated to the United States. In 1968, Ms. Rubinstein began her photographic career, briefly studying with Lisette Model, Jim Hughes and the late Diane Arbus. Her photographs have been published in many magazines and periodicals, including *ARTnews, Camera 35, Life, Look* and *The New York Times.* Two portfolios of her work, one of which includes an introduction by André Kertész, have been published by the Neikrug Gallery in New York. A monograph of her work was published by Morgan & Morgan in 1974. Ms. Rubinstein's photographs have been widely exhibited, including shows at the Library of Congress in Washington, D.C., the Metropolitan Museum of Art and International Center of Photography in New York, the Bibliothèque Nationale in Paris and the Israel Museum in Jerusalem. She has also taught at many photographic schools and workshops throughout the United States and Europe.

1. Minneapolis, 1979 2. Sister Virginia, 1979 3. Church, Italy, 1979
4. Monterey, 1977 5. Versailles, 1976

LUCE

HELEN BUTTFIELD

Photographing is a way of being in the world, of participating in the life of the world. The world exists outside of us, essentially indifferent; we live inside ourselves, alone.

I am amazed by the natural world. That it exists at all seems miracle enough, but that it does so with such unimaginable variety staggers the mind. It is beautiful, terrible, wonderfully strange.

When I photograph a tree, or a rock, or the ocean, I become for a moment part of that tree or that rock, I live in imagination the life of the sea. If I can fix their images clearly, all distinctions fall away and the sense of separateness is gone. When I really succeed the viewer disappears as well, and I wash my hands of the whole thing.

Helen Buttfield is a photographer, book designer and teacher of photography. An art historian by training and a naturalist by inclination, she was a painter before becoming a photographer. She has collaborated on four books which combine photography and poetry: "The Wind and the Rain," "The Park," "Of This World," and "The Way of Silence." Her photographs have appeared in *Look, Venture, Horizon, New York, The New York Herald-Tribune, Camera 35, Popular Photography, Time-Life Books* and in numerous photographic anthologies and books on natural history. She has exhibited at New York's Marcuse Pfeifer Gallery, Midtown Gallery, American Museum of Natural History, Lincoln Center for the Performing Arts, Floating Foundation of Photography and in many group shows. She teaches at the School of Visual Arts and is photographer-in-residence at the Center of Oriental Studies in New York.

1. Kapiti Island, 1967 2. Cherryplain, Winter, 1976 3. Cherryplain, Summer, 1975
4. Lake Benmore, 1966 5. Farewell Spit, 1967

This book has been set in Palatino and Caslon
by Logigraph Network Inc., New York, New York,
and was printed at the Morgan Press, Dobbs Ferry, New York.